T0194855

Upstream Teaching In The Church
A Transformative Teaching Method

THOMAS T. SHIELDS, SR. D MIN

WESTBOW
PRESS®
A DIVISION OF THOMAS NELSON
& ZONDERVAN

WestBow Press books may be ordered through booksellers or by contacting:

WestBow Press
A Division of Thomas Nelson & Zondervan
1663 Liberty Drive
Bloomington, IN 47403
www.westbowpress.com
1 (866) 928-1240

Scripture quotations are from the New Revised Standard Version Bible,
copyright © 1989 National Council of the Churches of Christ in the United
States of America. Used by permission. All rights reserved worldwide.

ISBN: 978-1-9736-7203-6 (sc)
ISBN: 978-1-9736-7204-3 (hc)
ISBN: 978-1-9736-7202-9 (e)

Library of Congress Control Number: 2019911739

Print information available on the last page.

WestBow Press rev. date: 9/3/2019

Contents

Author Acknowledgments

Before and during the process of writing this book, I considered with a great deal of seriousness what I was about to publicize. I was then and I am certain now that the issues I am addressing and the questions I am raising are crucial. I am equally certain that what I am advocating is sorely needed. Those who are open enough to give it thoughtful contemplation will without question discover a means of fashioning teaching in the church in a much more effective method. Not only will the satisfaction of those who teach be increased, I'm convinced that the learners themselves will demonstrate overwhelming gratitude. Because I have sensed a coveting for the method that I am advocating, I have purposely dedicated a great deal of time and effort in making sure the material I am presenting is well researched and accurate. Moreover, in the process of writing this book a lot of marvelous and sharing people were instrumental in helping me bring this project to life and fashioning it into the creation it has turned out to be. I would be remiss if I did not acknowledge with gratitude the case study participants who, through their participation, allowed me to peer into their struggles and experiences without censor. Their frank responses caused me to develop increased empathy for the learners who make up the various educational venues of our churches. While these participants came from a variety of different backgrounds and life experiences, they shared a common thirst for knowledge and desire to grow. Finally, I express my special gratitude to my helpers who have walked closely with me through the journey of making real this book, offering me their constant love, support, and, most of all, words of prayerful encouragement. To my friend and sister Ebony who has helped me realize so much about the power we all have within us to make things possible.

Introduction

In retrospect, I consider, the creation narrative found in Genesis to be the most appropriate analogy for the development which led to this endeavor to improve teaching in the Church setting, through the use of helping skills. In the beginning, it was just a notion "without form and void." The darkness of many of my unanswered questions was upon my shapeless concepts.

Among those many unanswered questions, there were a few that became paramount in my quest for an effective method to improve teaching in the Church setting. I needed to know:

How fashioning learners in the Church setting can become more personalized?

How can teachers develop skills necessary to relate to the interests of the learners?

How can teachers become familiar with the skills that are needed?

How can teachers enhance their creative abilities?

How can teachers be more facilitative in their fashioning efforts?

While this list was neither exhaustive in number nor conclusive in scope, they are representative of the core from which this book is fashioned. When I first raised these questions to knowledgeable practitioners, I had only a weak conception of the venture itself. Even as the light of formal research began to shine on my unanswered questions, it became obvious that my search would take me through several "creative" acts. Perhaps the most significant of these acts was my in- depth learning experience with the "Teaching-Learning Process" that I engaged in while pursuing my graduate degree at Union Theological Seminary. It was this exposure to the major concepts, skills, and strategies of teaching that first prompted me to look critically at traditional teaching efforts in the Church venues. At the same time, it enabled me to test out many of my own concepts about the roles of teachers in the Church setting. Moreover, this exposure also made it possible for me to discover, much to my extrication and satisfaction, that there were viable allies to my thinking. Among those, Robert R. Carkhuff and Bernard G. Berenson, Carl R. Rogers, Donald L. Griggs, Bruce Joyce and Marsha Weil, and of course, Dr. Sarah Little. It was this combination of academic studies combined with my passion and experience for Christian education that served above all, as the core catalyst for the eventual formulations of my endeavor.

Not only have I emerge from these endeavors with solid foundations on which to further develop my understanding of the theory and practice of teaching in the church, but more especially I now feel more confident that "new creations" of improved teaching efforts will take place. Much of my original naiveté has been replaced not only with conclusive answers, however. On the contrary, I have learned the very hard lessons that are echoed by many experts in the field of education but are best stated by Robert J. Schaefer in his foreword to the first edition to Joyce and Weil's book, "Models of Teaching". His conclusion that "...there is no royal freeway to pedagogical success, no painless solution to complex instructional problems, and no future in our persistent effort to describe 'best teaching practice'"[1] still impels me today.

---

[1] Bruce Joyce and Marsha Weil, Models of Teaching, (Englewood Cliffs, New Jersey: Prentice-Hall, Inc., 1980), p. XIX.

I

Motivations for Moving Upstream

Developing a Critical Consciousness of Chaos in the Classroom

"The earth was a formless void and darkness covered the face of the Deep Genesis 1:2a

Where there is a lack of learning in our church's Christian Education venues, confusion thrives and chaos abounds in the minds of learners. Yet, recognizing a lack of clearness and relevance in todays' teaching methods will not thoroughly uncover or address the chaos or confusion in our learner's psyches. This is true despite the fact that on any given day, in any given classroom, in the minds of learners in our churches, various forms of bewilderment and perplexity exists (Anxiety, depression, phobias, etc.). As lessons are

1

presented a skilled and attentive teacher can hear it, feel it and even see it on the learner's faces. The tragedy is however, learners experiencing this chaos frequently leave our church's classrooms the same way they came.

The account of creation in Genesis reveals our Creator's attentive awareness of existing chaos and bareness which subsequently led to creative actions (Genesis 1:1-4). The same must be the motivation for our teaching "Upstream" in the church. Those who desire to teach effectively in the church would especially need to develop a similar awareness regarding the outcomes of "traditional" teaching in order for "Upstream Teaching" to become an imperative. Consequently, there needs to be a concise awareness of how current methods of teaching in the church have evolved and why the results are far less effective.

In his book entitled "how to be the best Christian study group leader" "How to Be the Best Christian Study Group Leader," Israel Galindo deals extensively with this issue of sterility in our teaching. He, in fact has some rather strong words to say about the ineffectiveness of traditional teaching. Galindo says:

"I call it "the deadly null expectancy factor." By this phrase I mean the ways we often teach in our congregations ensure that Christians have no expectation of actually learning anything, or if they do learn something, they have no expectation that what they learn will have direct application to their lives – at work, at home, or on a personal level.[2]

Not only does Galindo deride traditional teaching methods for their inability to create a sense of expectancy in our learners, he is obviously not mild in characterizing the results as "lethal" in terms of its usefulness to learners. So, on the one hand, heightening awareness in those of us who teach in the church is crucial. On the other hand, because it could take us in several different directions, I will narrow the probe by simply pointing out certain brief yet compelling details, I believe to be relevant.

To begin with, most of us who teach in the church will agree that our commission to teach was given by Jesus (Matthew 28:20a). Yet, todays' implementation involves distinctions that were not mandated by him. For example, when it comes to deciding which persons make the best teachers, it is not an uncomplicated task. Experts seem to agree that good teachers are actually

---

[2] Donald L. Griggs, Teachin9 Teachers to Teach, (Liver- more, Ca.: Griggs Educational Service, 1974), p. 1.

"made, not born." They also seem to agree that some teachers possess more "gifted" ability than others. At the same time, other experts contend that the task of teaching is not a static one. In other words, they suggest that we tend to avoid the use of certain fixed principles when we teach. On the contrary, as noted Christian educator, Donald Griggs points out, "teaching is an art that must be developed, practiced, and evaluated for its effectiveness."[3] What Griggs means by this is the quality, as well as the shape of our teaching efforts in the church continues to be in a state of development. To put it more bluntly, unless teachers persistently acquire skills needed to improve our teaching, we are destined to be ineffective. [4]

Still, identifying effective teachers does not eliminate the absolute necessity to accomplish it (accomplish what? Find a word to concisely restate the point carried over from the previous paragraph). So although

---

[3] Jack L. Seymour and Donald E. Miller with Sarah P. Little, Charles R. Foster, Allen J. Moore and Carol A. Wehrheim, Contemporary Approaches to Christian Education, (Nashville: Abingdon, 1982), p. 39.

[4] Joyce and Weil, Models of Teaching, p. 1. 5Sam Adams and John L. Garrett, Jr., To Be A Teacher (Englewood Cliffs, New Jersey: Prentice-Hall, Inc., 1969), p. 129

there appears to be no general agreement on a particular definition, some Christian educators have formulated definitions mainly for pragmatic reasons.

Noted professors of Christian Education, Sarah Little, for example, borrowing from Thomas Green's approach to instruction has formulated that:

> "Teaching is the process of dealing with subject matter in such a way as to enable students to assess the truth of the same in terms of their own frames of reference."[5]

Bruce Joyce and Marsha Weil, on the other hand, see teaching as:

> "A process by which teacher and student create a shared environment including sets of values and beliefs (agreements about what is important) which, in turn, color their view of reality."[6]

---

[5] Sam Adams and John L. Garrett, Jr., To Be A Teacher (Englewood Cliffs, New Jersey: Prentice-Hall, Inc., 1969), p. 129.

[6] Ibid., p. 129

Again, it is not my intent to offer an exhaustive list of definitions but merely to demonstrate the abundance of definitions to those who are reluctant to look critically at our current teaching methods. In my view, regardless of venue, teaching is more accurately defined by its purpose.

Making such an assertion however, not only requires us, to look critically at traditional teaching/learning. It becomes necessary to take note of modern day expansions. For instance, when we examine the history of secular education, (from which modern day Christian Education methods came, it is apparent that early concepts of learning demanded teaching goals that focused heavily upon student's ability to merely master information. Thus, it also becomes apparent that:

In the minds of many early teachers, the process of teaching did consist of essentially imparting information. An example would be the teaching of Latin in a Grammar School. The goal was simple, since mastery of Latin was the prime concern. This made the teaching operation almost entirely a recurring cycle of drill, recite, drill, recite.[7]

---

[7] Lindley J. Stiles and Mattie F. Dorsey, *Democratic Teaching in Secondary Schools*, (Chicago: J. B. Lippincott Company, 1950), p. 430.

An examination of the textbooks of the Latin Grammar era, such as "Cheever's Accidence," supports this conclusion. Such teaching goals as understanding, analysis, or synthesis received little or no attention.

Goals of this teaching method are understandable when it is also understood that the expectation is principally the learner's ability to reproduce or recall the material studied. On the other hand, because this type of learning does not require reflective thinking, the teaching process even in the church became fixed and static. When compared to many modern day concepts of teaching, one can safely say that the learning effects of early teaching forms were minimal and the instructional benefits were generally restrictive. That is say:

...The objective was chiefly one of memorization. Hence, the process of teaching was limited to those steps that would promote such learning[8].

Therefore we can see that the goals of early teaching in the church definitely did not have among its fundamental purposes, the desire to meet the needs and interests of the learner. On the contrary, such displays as curiosity and creativeness were discouraged

---

[8] Bruce Joyce and Marsha Weil, Models of Teaching, (Engle- wood Cliffs, New Jersey: Prentice-Hall, Inc., 1980), p. 22.

or treated on many occasions as disciplinary problems. So it was not uncommon for early teachers, regardless of venue, to spend more time engaged in maintaining discipline than actually engaging in instruction. For example:

As applied in early colonial schools, this meant that the schoolmaster, in addition to being able to out-spell and out-translate his pupils, had to possess the physical strength and ability to 'thrash' any student who failed to submit to instructions or to master his lessons.[9]

It should be noted, too, that the colonial religious schools as well as the secular were direct transplants from European nations to their colonies in the New World. Since European society was despotic in character, it was to be expected that teaching methods would similarly be characterized by autocratic procedures. At the same time, teaching in the early schools was a direct outgrowth of a narrowly conceived purpose; namely, the development of literacy for a select portion of colonial youth. As a matter of fact, the early schools did not accept the responsibility for preparing youth for life, since this was considered a duty of the home.

[9] Paulo Freire, Pedagogy Of the Oppressed, (New York: The Continuum publishing Corporation, 1981), p. 58.

Notwithstanding, the objectives and goals of teaching in the early schools emphasized the memorization of logically organized bodies of knowledge, with the training of the mind and the conformity to adult standards of scholarship and academic discipline. Hence, Christian Education inherited a background of autocratic teaching methods, which continued to follow the leadership of authoritarian schools in Europe until well into the twentieth century. In fact, much of the autocratic practices in Christian education and teaching today can be traced directly to either our original inheritance of despotic schools or to our later imitation of educational practices in schools of despotic nations. Moreover, it is apparent, when one examines the teaching process and techniques in a variety of venues, including the church today, for "many people, conveying information is the primary business of the school..."[10]

It should also be apparent that, for many modern day teachers, in the church the teaching task is very much like that of his or her colonial counterpart. The public educational system of America today from

---

[10] ibid. p. 58.

kindergarten to university and from which teaching in the church originated is flooded with examples of what Paulo Freire calls the "banking concept" of education. Such a concept involves:

Narration (with the teacher as narrator) leads the students to memorize mechanically the narrated content. Worst yet it turns them into 'containers into 'receptacles' to be 'filled' by the teacher. The more completely he fills the receptacles, the better a teacher he is. The more meekly the receptacles permit themselves to be filled, the better students they are.[11]

One may argue that Freire's reference is purely Latin American. However, when one realizes that Latin America experienced much of the same cultural and education inheritance as North America, it is not difficult to see how it also manifests some of the same autocratic educational procedures. As in the case of Latin America, in North America:

Education thus becomes an act of depositing in which the students are the depositories and the teacher is the depositor. Instead of communicating, the teacher

---

[11] Carl R. Rogers, Freedom To Learn for the 80's, (Columbus: Charles E. Merrill Publishing Company, 1983), p. 17.

issues communiqués and makes deposits, which the students patiently receive, memorize, and repeat.[12]

While Freire's views of the goals of teaching in Latin America similar to the teaching goals in North America, those goals have recently undergone considerable expansion. Although the emphasis on memorization and imparting information still remain essential to the teaching process, educators have become increasingly aware of the learner's need to be more perceptual. This awareness to move from autocratic educational procedures is expressed vividly by Carl Rogers in his book, "Freedom To learn."

It would seem that to most people, teaching involves keeping order in the class, pouring forth facts, usually through lectures or textbooks, giving examinations, and setting grades. This stereotype is badly in need of overhauling.[13]

This need for an expanded approach to the teaching task is further echoed by Stanford Erickson in his book, "Motivation for Learning."

We need new words for 'teaching'; words that say

---

[12] Stanford C. Ericksen, Motivation for Learninq, (Ann Arbor: The University of Michigan Press, 1974), p. 1

[13] Carl R. Rogers, Freedom to Learn for the 80, p. 18.

more about why and how a student learns and remembers, how his attitude changes and his values take shape. The new language about teaching must offer greater detail about conditions for learning: how ambitions are stirred; how some anxieties are lessened and new ones generated: how the store of information in memory grows; by what process old labels acquire new meaning; how abstract concepts are formed, generalizations tested and value judgments explored; how attitudes are sharpened as new knowledge is examined and combined with what the student already knows. Finally, the language of teaching must deal with the processes the student uses to clarify his own picture of who he is, what he is doing and where he is going--solo and as a member of society. [14]

In short, educators are beginning to recognize the need to include the all-important aspects of student's needs and interests into their teaching goals. It also appears that concerns for student's individual differences, as opposed to narrow homogeneous concerns are becoming a part of teaching goals. Teachers are now accepting the idea that students are inherently

---

[14] F. Robert Paulsen, *American Education*, (Tucson, Arizona: The University of Arizona Press, 1967), p.83.

active, creative and curious. It is my belief that this evolved approach toward more meaningful content and personalized teaching should also be applied to teaching in the church.

Understanding Traditional Teaching in the Church

God said, "Let There Be Light"

"Just as "light" is the means employed in Genesis (1:3a) to dispel the darkness; understanding our current teaching methods in the church, must be the course for clearing the way to creativity. Hence, teaching in the church must proceed from a clear understanding of what currently happens to learners during the lesson presentation and what needs to occur as we move upstream.

It is vital that we acknowledge the early goals of teaching have already expanded to show that:

The primary task of the teacher is to permit the student to learn, to feed his or her own curiosity. Merely to absorb facts is of only slight value in the present, and usually of even less value in the future. Learning how to learn is the element that is always of value, now and in the future. Thus, the teacher's task is delicate, demanding, and a truly exalted calling. In true teaching there is no place for the authoritarian, nor the person who is on an 'ego trip'.

As the goals of teaching are being expanded, so has the definition of what it means to be a teacher. Thus, modern day teaching is becoming a radical departure from its early conceptualization.

In expanding the goals of teaching, educators have also found it necessary to reexamine the meaning of learning. Without attempting to survey the vast number of "laws" of learning, it is safe to say that early definitions of learning were characterized by the three "d's", disciplined, difficult, and dreadful. Making learning too easy was often construed as a disservice to the student. Since ease diminished the amount of pain, it was felt that the less pain that the student endured, the less learning would occur. Modern definitions of learning take exception to this view, however.

As educators, we know that the opportunities to grow and develop are directly related to the extent to which a person can give his self and his wholeness to any learning situation. While it is true that for some people learning may require labor and considerable effort, it should not--and indeed cannot--be measured by its painfulness.

It can also be said of early definitions of learning that since the emphasis was heavily upon memorization, learning consequently was dominated by mental discipline. Proponents of a learning concept that involves mental discipline view the mind as being mainly comparable to a muscle. Thus as it is with most muscles, there is a need for strenuous exercise in order to develop them. It was assumed by these proponents that the development of the mind could only be achieved by having students wrestle with extremely difficult subject matter. Often this meant that the element of practicality was of little concern. The chief criterion was learning had to be difficult.

In addition, there were those whose view of learning as punishment created much fear and dread. Such a view contained a rather unique twist, since one of the weapons most often used by teachers was the requirement to put in extra study times in spelling and arithmetic.

Consider for example, the teacher who doubles the assignment to 'reward' misbehavior. Some teachers have even gone so far as to design special assignments for individual students, the length of each being determined by how bad he has been. Other manifestations of this attitude are orders such as: 'stay after school for an hour of study time', 'stay in during recess'.

It is obvious why students learned to dislike those subjects that were used to punish them. Moreover, it was inevitable that the harshness and narrowness of this concept of learning often proved to be counter-productive. Learning in this instance served mostly the goals-paternalism and conformity rather than preparing students for life.

Ironically so, many modern educators still hold to naive assumptions that learning is essentially mental discipline properly and intentionally inflicted by the teacher. Learning of this type was by design, "teacher centered" because it was directed towards producing those responses which the teacher arbitrarily determined were proper and important. Little effort, if any, was made to focus on the abilities, interests and attitudes of the students themselves.

II

The Motivations for Moving Upstream

A. The Inadequacy of Contemporary Methods

To begin it must be grasped by all who are concerned that any appraisal of contemporary teaching methods on the basis for improving learning in the Church setting must out necessity proceed from a concise understanding of what is deemed to be "contemporary" teaching in the Church. Granted such an endeavor may advance from several different vantage points. However, I cannot over emphasize that certain presuppositions must be considered germane to the conclusions that I will draw.

For example, it is generally agreed among Christian educators that effective teachers are made, not born, although some may possess more unique teaching ability than others. At the same time, it is generally agreed that the act or task of teaching is not a static one, practiced according to certain fixed principles. On the contrary, as Donald Griggs so aptly puts it, "teaching is an art that must be developed, practiced and evaluated for its effectiveness".[15] This means then, the quality and shape of our teaching efforts in the church are always in a state of "not yet-ness". Stated differently, when skills needed to improve our teaching efforts are acquired by us, we are thus prepared to teach more effectively.

From such a conclusion, it follows that the question, "what is the contemporary method of teaching in the church?" should logically be raised. From the outset however, it must be understood that unlike the quality and shape of teaching outside the church setting, general agreement by educators on what is teaching in the church is nonexistent. In fact an established definition for teaching especially in the church has and continues to be an elusive goal. Still, the elusiveness of a definition has not in any way deterred attempts to formulate one. While not generally agreeing on a

---

[15] Sam Adams and John L. Garrett, Jr., To Be A Teacher, p. 223

particular definition for widespread use, most Christian educators seemed to have formulated a definition for pragmatic reasons.

Sarah Little, for example, borrowing from Thomas Green's approach to instruction has formulated that:

Teaching is the process of dealing with subject matter in such a way as to enable students to assess the truth of the same in terms of their own frames of reference.[16]

Bruce Joyce and Marsha Weil, on the other hand, see teaching as:

> *A process by which teacher and student create a shared environment including sets of values and be beliefs (agreements about what is important) which, in turn, color their view of reality.[17]*

It is not my intent to offer here an exhaustive list of definitions by educators of what teaching in the church is but merely to substantiate the viability of definitions of teaching for practical reasons. For purely

---

[16] F. Robert Paulsen, *American Education*, p.83.

[17] F. Robert Paulsen, *American Education*, p.18.

pragmatic reasons then, I submit that teaching in the church setting is usually more accurately defined by its goals. In making such a proposal however, it becomes necessary, first of all, to look critically at traditional implications of learning and secondly, to take note of its modern- day expansion.

B. Encounters When We Appraise Teaching "Historically?"

It is apparent from an analysis of traditional concepts of learning that teaching goals which focused heavily upon student's ability to master information justified the method that teachers in the church employed.

Hence like teachers in the secular school:

In the minds of many early teachers, the process of teaching did consist of essentially imparting information. An example would be the teaching of Latin in a Grammar School. The goal was simple, since mastery of Latin was the prime concern. This made the teaching operation almost entirely a recurring cycle of drill, recite, drill, recite.[18]

An examination of the textbooks of the Latin

---

[18] Locke E. Bowman, Jr., Teaching Today, (Philadelphia: (The Westminister Press, 1980), p. 93.

Grammar era, such as Cheever's Accidence, supports this conclusion. Such teaching goals as understanding, analysis, or synthesis received little or no attention.[19]

Goals of this type are understandable when it is also understood that the expected result was principally the learner's ability to reproduce or recall the material studied. On the other hand, because this type of learning does not require reflective thinking in order to respond, the teaching process was essentially fixed and static. When compared to many modern day concepts of teaching in the church, one can safely say that the nurturant effects of early teaching forms were minimal and the instructional effects were generally restrictive. That is:

> The objective was chiefly one of memorization. Hence, the process of teaching was limited to those steps that would promote such learning.[20]

Recently, however, educators have recognized the need to make learning more "student centered". This

---

[19] Ibid., p. 94.

[20] Ibid., p. 95.

change in focus has come to mean first of all, that, before students can learn effectively, they must be in a mood to learn. In other words, they must be receptive or motivated to learning and they must have some reason for learning. As opposed to the view that the more painful, the more learning takes place; the greater pleasure encountered in the learning experience, the greater the level of achievement. Consequently, it has been realized by educators that the greatest potential for learning exists in the student's response to a given subject. This means the teacher has a responsibility to lessen the psychological pain undergone in the learning experience; not to increase it.

Secondly, this change in focus has come to mean that teachers must find some way of structuring realization into the learning experience. This may often come about by the teacher's favorable comment on the student's achievement. The learner whose tastes of success have been slight or non-existent needs to develop habits of comprehending and succeeding. Hence, learning must be augmented by several methods of employing reinforcement. When timed correctly, reinforcement not only encourages desired student responses, it makes those responses more likely in subsequent behavior.

Finally, these changes in focus have come to mean that teachers must ensure that learning involves the quality of being applicable or pertinent to the learner's maturity. Thus, learning must address itself to the questions—why and how? If the student perceives what is being learned as relevant to his or her interests or needs, the odds for learning are increased considerably. On the other hand, if there seems to be no justification other than a demand for right answers, the student's learning will be minimizes if not made much more difficult. One may note that when learning becomes more relevant to the lives of learner, teachers may occasionally find previous arbitrary selections made by them proving to be embarrassing. Occasionally, it will be discovered that some previous certainties will be difficult if not impossible to justify. Educators have come to the realization that the opportunities to grow and develop are directly related to the extent to which students can give themselves to the learning experience. Moreover, educators have recently become more aware that 'learning is achieved when a person undergoes a change within by means of discovering his or her own resources and capacities.When learning has no meaning, however, it is difficult to achieve and easily forgotten. Therefore, when some modern educators talk about the definition of learning, it is, in the words of Carl Rogers:

> *"not the lifeless, sterile, futile quickly forgotten stuff that is crammed into the mind of the poor helpless individual tied into his seat by ironclad bonds of conformity!... Such learning involves the mind only. It is learning that takes place 'from the neck up.' It does not involve feelings or personal meanings; it has no relevance for the whole person.*[21]

In contrast to that learning which is based on the elements that have meaning for the teacher only (teacher centered), a growing number of proponents are contending that the teacher must enable the student to learn in such a way that learning has significance and meaning for him or her. To be able to do this, however, the teacher must possess and be able to use effectively those helping skills that will enable him or her to become one "who actualizes student

[21] Seymour, Miller, Little, Forster, Moore, Wehrheim, Contemporary Approaches to Christian Education, p. 38.

potential" - a facilitator of a person-centered approach to education. In short, the educator of today must become a teacher-facilitator.

Without question, the demand for teachers to possess interpersonal and problem-solving skills is increasing in secular and Christian education. Studies have documented that student achievement is significantly higher when the teacher is a helper-teacher. In one example where educators were evaluated based upon student results and the level of teacher emotional and interpersonal skills, it was noted that:

In summary, these studies suggested that the heart of helping involved the emotional and interpersonal changes in the helpee that were brought about differentially by the helper's emotional and interpersonal skills. The work suggested a number of new studies generalizing the effects to other areas of helpee functioning.[22]

The earliest of these generalization studies was done by Aspy (1969) in the educational realm, Aspy selected teachers functioning at high and low levels of emotional and inter-personal skills and assessed their effects on the intellectual achievement of elementary

---

[22] Ibid., p. 38.

school students. Thus, he studied the helper-teacher dimensions and their effects upon the helpee-learner's intellectual functioning. What Aspy found was consistent with previous work. In general the students of high functioning teachers achieved at significantly higher levels than students of low functioning teachers on a variety of communication and computation skills.[23]

The effective teacher of today may constantly find themselves in the role of helper-teacher. The two roles to a large extent are inseparable, especially to the teacher whose focus is "student centered" and whose goals are to be a facilitator of learning and one who actualizes student potential.

Particulars that make "Teaching" in the Church unique?

As in the case of teaching in the secular setting, teaching in the Church is not simple to define. There are those such as Locke E. Bowman who, borrowing from Jerome Bruner's "Toward a Theory of Instruction" would say it is activating. Bowman, then, sees the

---

[23] Ibid., p. 41.

teachers in the Church setting as being those who are initiators or activators of creative acts, which he considered to be learning. According to Bowman:

They are present to help something to begin, to sprout, to take its first breath. Like midwives they are not fully responsible for the process, but they are as close to it as they can get. By being present, they can play a role in activating.[24]

To play a part in causing something important to begin in full recognition that one is not wholly responsible for what went before and for what will come-that is what is meant by activating.[25]

Hence, according to Bowman, when the teachers take initiative in raising questions, posing dilemmas and presenting problems which in turn causes students to see alternative possibilities, varieties of answers to questions; several ways of solving a posed problem or dilemma and their curiosity is aroused the goal is reached. The best example of this, in Bowman's view is the use of parables by Jesus.

The parables do offer alternatives that we can

---

[24] Ibid., p. 42.

[25] Sarah Little, Learning Together in the Christian Fellow- ship, (Richmond, Virginia: John Knox Press, 1956), p. 22.

continue to explore. They raise just the right amount of uncertainty so that our curiosity is stimulated. We puzzle over them in such a way that we learn. We are led to the creation of a lasting image of the Kingdom of God.[26]

What Bowman is suggesting is that teachers in the Church setting are indeed facilitators of learning what it means to be Christ-like. Not however, by simply dictating what that is in their view or giving out so called "right" answers which they expect students to memorize. Rather they are to help students to probe for their own answers and discover for themselves these images of the Kingdom of God.

There are others such as Dr. Sarah Little, who defines our teaching in the Church setting as religious instruction that is carried out in the context of a particular religious community and that it takes its orientation from the purposes, language beliefs, and self-understanding of that community. While Sarah uses the term "religious" she makes it clear that for her Christian is the better term. Like Bowman, she rejects a definition which portrays our teaching efforts as "a kind of brainwashing, an unreflective 'passing on' of

---

[26] Ibid., p. 16.

static propositions to be received as doctrine". What is also clear from Dr. Little's definition is that the teacher must accept the responsibility for the content of that is communicated to the learner but not whether or not it will be accepted. In other words, it cannot be the objective or purposing of our teaching efforts in the Church setting to manufacture Christians as some evangelistic denominations seem to press for. Instead, the sum total of our teaching efforts can only put before the learners a gospel with such an understanding and clarity that those efforts will, in turn, confront them with the need to make a decision.

According to Dr. Little:

> *It is a process of exploring the church's tradition and self-understanding in such a way that persons can understand, assess, and therefore respond to the truth of the gospel for themselves.*[27]

What I see that is implicit in Dr. Little's definition is the imperatives of self-determination for the learner

---

[27] Sarah Little, Learning Together in the Christian Fellow- ship, (Richmond, Virginia: John Knox Press, 1956), p. 22.

to arrive at conclusions and to make those responses frm them that will transform his or her life. It is also clear that the image in her mind of teaching in the Church setting does not involve the efforts of trained experts who can provide the learner with all the answers, but those of typical lay-persons. As she puts it:

I have no zeal for the "unprofessionalizing" of teaching. Many volunteer Sunday school teachers, admitting that they do not know, explore with sincerity and diligence the gospel they seek to understand. They explain too, with clarity, sometimes greater than those of us who are caught up in the jargon of the day, or who are more concerned with impressing our peers than with being clear.[28]

What I also see from both Dr. Little and Bowman is the tension that must be maintained between the Church setting teacher's responsibility to facilitate discernment and understanding and the teacher's recognition that what has been initiated through his or her teaching efforts can only find its culmination in the grace and mercy of God. This is not only true of the evangelistic efforts of teachers in the Church setting

---

[28] Ibid., p. 25.

but it is equally true of its efforts to facilitate Christian nurture.

God said, "Let There Be Light"

Understanding Traditional Teaching in the Church

"Just as "light" is the means employed in Genesis (1:3a) to bring dispel the darkness; understanding our current teaching methods in the church, must be the course for clearing the way to creativity. Hence, teaching in the church must proceed from a clear understanding of what currently happens and what needs to occur as we move upstream.

The early goals of teaching have already begun to be more expanded to show that:

The primary task of the teacher is to permit the student to learn, to feed his or her own curiosity. Merely to absorb facts is of only slight value in the present, and usually of even less value in the future. Learning how to learn is the element that is always of value, now and in the future. Thus, the teacher's task is delicate, demanding, and a truly exalted calling. In true teaching there is no place for the authoritarian, nor the person who is on an 'ego trip'.

As the goals of teaching are being expanded, so has the definition of what it means to be a teacher. Thus, modern day teaching is becoming a radical departure from its early conceptualization.

In expanding the goals of teaching, educators have also found it necessary to reexamine the meaning of learning. Without attempting to survey the vast number of "laws" of learning, it is safe to say that early definitions of learning were characterized by the three "d's", disciplined, difficult, and dreadful. Making learning too easy was often construed as a disservice to the student. Since ease diminished the amount of pain, it was felt that the less pain that the student endured, the less learning would occur. Modern definitions of learning take exception to this view, however.

As educators, we know that the opportunities to grow and develop are directly related to the extent to which a person can give his self and his wholeness to any learning situation. While it is true that for some people learning may require labor and considerable effort, it should not, and indeed cannot, be measured by its painfulness.

It can also be said of early definitions of learning that since the emphasis was heavily upon memorization, learning consequently was dominated by mental discipline. Proponents of a learning concept that involves mental discipline view the mind as being mainly comparable to a muscle. Thus as it is with most muscles, there is a need for strenuous exercise in order to develop them. It was assumed by these proponents that the development of the mind could only be achieved by having students wrestle with extremely difficult subject matter. Often this meant that the element of practicality was of little concern. The chief criterion was learning had to be difficult.

In addition, there were those whose view of learning as punishment created much fear and dread. Such a view contained a rather unique twist, since one of the weapons most often used by teachers was the requirement to put in extra study times in spelling and arithmetic.

Consider for example, the teacher who doubles the assignment to 'reward' misbehavior. Some teachers have even gone so far as to design special assignments for individual students, the length of each being determined by how bad he has been. Other manifestations of this attitude are orders such as: 'stay after school for an hour of study time', 'stay in during recess'.

It is obvious why students learned to dislike those

subjects that were used to punish them. Moreover, it was inevitable that the harshness and narrowness of this concept of learning often proved to be counter-productive. Learning in this instance served mostly the goals-paternalism and conformity rather than preparing students for life.

Ironically, so many modern educators still hold to naive assumptions that learning is essentially mental discipline properly and intentionally inflicted by the teacher. Learning of this type was by design, "teacher centered" because it was directed towards producing those responses, which the teacher arbitrarily determined were proper and important. Little effort, if any, was made to focus on the abilities, interests and attitudes of the students themselves.

The Imperative of Christian Nurture

Without question, teaching in the Church setting must concern itself with the nurture of persons belonging to the Christian community in all of their relationships and throughout their lifespans. At the same time, the emergence of noted "evangelists" clearly reveal that there have been and still are times in the church's teaching history when it has been guilty of a one sided emphasis in favor of soul-winning. Even today, examples of so called, "evangelical congregations" suggests that the church is not completely purged of the neglect of its responsibility to facilitate Christian growth and nurture. Pastors obviously get more validation and increases in compensation from growth in numbers than growth in emotional and behavioral maturity.

In his book entitled "Changes That Heal" Dr. Henry Cloud says, "every week I see Christians who are suffering from a whole range of emotional problems: anxiety, loneliness, grief over broken relationships, resentment, and feelings of inadequacy. Often they have been struggling with these problems for years. They are people in pain."[29]

According to Cloud, the help offered to Christians in emotional pain over the years has done untold damage and has led many to reach the conclusion Job did: "You smear me with lies; you are worthless physicians, all of you! If only you would be altogether silent! For you, that would be wisdom"(Job 13:4 – 5)." [30]

---

[29] Ibid., p. 9.

[30] Frank E. Dunn, The Ministering Teacher, (Valley Forge: Judson Press, 1982), p. 33.

Because the answers coming from the church are often vague and confusing Cloud says, "Faced with this kind of help, sufferers either learn to fake healing to remain in the church, or leave the church, deciding that their faith provides little solace for their emotional pain."[31]

Still, no church can truly exemplify its teaching responsibility without that balance brought about by the inclusion of its responsibility for providing the members of its community with opportunities for consolation and growth. As T. Franklin Miller puts it:

> *All growing things need cultivation, care, food, water; in short, they need nurture. Whenever one surrenders to Christ in full commitment of his life and his nature partakes of the divine nature, there is a difference in the quality of his relationship to God; but prior to, during and forever following such a great decision, there must be the nurture and support of the Christian community.*[32]

---

[31] Paul H. Vieth, How To Teach In The Church setting, (Philadelphia: The Westminister Press, 1935), p. 10.

[32] Frank E. Dunn, The Ministering Teacher, p. 81.

At this point a word needs to be said about the characteristics of those who teach in our churches. For anyone who is in anyway cognizant of the magnitude of the task is also aware that those persons who assume such a task are shouldering grave responsibility.

The question, of course, is what kind of person are we talking about? In answering such a probing question we need, from the outset, to dispel any notions of religious pompousness. We are not even describing ordinarily accomplished Bible scholars. We are, however, speaking of persons who are established members of the Christian community and are reasonably competent and confident in the faith he or she is articulating. Most of all we are talking about persons who attempt with integrity to teach by example.

In the words of T. Franklin Miller:

> "a teacher cannot give his faith to anyone, since faith is a part of one's own response to God. At the same time, it must be recognized that one teaches as much by what he is as by what he says. A radiant, vital, vibrant faith in God is as contagious as measles, and somebody is going to catch it when

> *he is exposed to it in the life of a skilled and dedicated teacher."* [33]

Miller's point is obviously well grasped by most who teach as well as those who are responsible for teaching teachers. For example, Dr. Sarah P. Little puts it this way:

God's ultimate revelation is that of a Person speaking to persons. God incarnate in Jesus Christ, the 'Word made flesh' spoke and speaks in action and in Being. Somehow, when a person meets Jesus Christ, all that he is and does speaks to other men of this Christ and enables them to meet Him, too. [34]

Another relevant point Dr. Little makes is "...truth is communicated through persons, through what they are and how they act, as well as through words and ideas." [35] In speaking of the persons who teach in the church I have not attempted here to be thorough or conclusive in enumerating the characteristics of those who teach in the church. At the same time, I consider

---

[33] Robert W. Lynn and Elliott Wright, The Big Little School, (Birmingham, Alabama: Religious Education Press, 1980), p. 24.

[34] Ibid.

[35] Ibid., p.35.

it imperative to point out that whatever is teaching in the church must be defined by who is actually doing the teaching.

Too often the tasks of recruiting and maintaining a high skill level of those who teach in the church is taken casually and without due consideration. Furthermore, rarely if ever is continuing education or teacher training deemed a requirement for teachers in the church setting. When it is done the training facilitator's competency is usually minimal and based upon cost rather than proficiency.

The end result is often failure as well as disappointment. Moreover the damage done to both the students and the teacher is usually very severe. The miracle is that we still do so much with so little; both in terms of the quantity of dedicated people, funds allocated and the time allotted.

Despite numerous examples even in some of our largest churches that suggests the teaching ministry of the church is optional, without question the commission issued by Jesus contains evidence to the contrary. Hence,

The church has no option in its teaching ministry. The church may choose who will teach, what will be taught' to whom, and where and when; it does not choose whether or not it will educate. In the very nature of its being and its mission the church is called to engage in education,[36]

These words of T. Franklin Miller describe unambiguously the mandate that we have for our teaching efforts. In view of the over-whelming nature of our mission as a Christian community, as well as the implicit nature of the commission given by Jesus to "... teach them" the question, why do we teach? May correctly be answered by asking, how can we do other- wise? Frank E. Dunn in his book "The Ministering Teacher" draws the analogy of vessels with many cracks filled by wax as being typical of the lives of those persons we teach in the Church setting.[37] The danger being the fact that lives like vessels must be able to withstand heat and pressure. According to Dunn:

Our major responsibility in Christian education is to guide people into the process of building their vessels without wax, that is, to develop a sincere faith which will, along with the pure heart and clear conscience,

---

[36] Ibid.,p.63.

[37] Ibid., p. 63.

produce the love the church is talking about but seldom evidences.[38]

There are obviously many reasons we can give for our teaching efforts in the church. Among those however, the needs that lead to wholeness and maturity are very close to being, if not paramount. Without question our teaching efforts presuppose that our learners have some deficiency which we believe we can address. In the words of Paul H. Vieth:

> *The teacher undertakes to help the pupil to acquire the learning which he needs. He does this in the confidence that he possesses some knowledge or skill through which he may guide the pupil into a richer life. Unless the pupil has some need which may be met, there is no ground for teaching him. Unless the teacher can, in some way, help the pupil to richer and fuller living, he is of no value as a teacher.*[39]

---

[38] Paul Tillich, Systematic Theology, VoL I (Chicago: The University of Chicago Press, 1951), p. 6.

[39] Marvin J. Taylor, ed An Introduction to Christian Education, (Nashville: Abingdon Press, 1966), p. 36.

To underscore Vieth's words, we can say with confidence that our motives for teaching must be to a very large extent in response to the fact that all members of the Christian community fall short of the goals of a "richer and fuller living".

Exploring the Biblical Models

When we take into account the whole of Scripture, we are able to see that there are numerous models from both the New and the Old Testament that we can draw from.

In the Old Testament the word (law-mad) to teach and to do so skillfully is used several times by the Deuteronomic writer (Deut. 4:10, 14; 5:31; 11:19; 20:18; 31:19) as an imperative to teach for the purpose of remembering the providence of God and the covenant relationship which He had established with His people. It must be pointed out here that even though teaching appears to be little more than the processing of information and learning the act of memorization, the two were also acts from whom faith in Yahweh's continued providence was communicated. This word which is also found in Chronicles, the Psalms, Job,

Jeremiah, and Daniel, does not provide us with the only Old Testament model but it appears to be the most frequently used.

In the New Testament (didasko) is the word that is most often used. It is this word that is used in describing the opening of the teaching ministry of Jesus (Mk. 6:2), and it is the same word which is used in his farewell discourse which is commonly described as the "great commission". (...teaching them...Mat. 28:20). It has been said repeatedly that no one has ever equaled Jesus in his teaching ability or his method. This is particularly true of his use of parables. As Lock E. Bowman has pointed out to us the example of Jesus is a model, a facilitator, activator, creator of learning par-excellence. Still, it was his commission to those followers that he left behind, to perpetuate his teaching ministry that looms largely from the accounts in the Book of Acts of the growth and development of the early church. It is this model of a teaching ministry that is responsible both for communicating the faith and Christian maturity that we can draw from today. Notwithstanding it is an outgrowth of that which has its beginnings with the "master" teacher himself. Thus:

If we understand that all Christians are summoned

to a vocation of ministry (or service), then that ministry is properly viewed as an extension of the working of Jesus Christ. He is making all things new; and that creative work of our Lord, in which we are co-laborers fundamentally, involves teaching.[40]

The Traditional Concepts

Any serious discussion of the traditional models that we use to teach in the church today must take into consideration the many images that teaching the church has had over the years. When one examines those images, it appears that Ellis Nelson was right in suggesting that teaching in the Church setting is what people think it is.

The originators of the "Sunday School" movement apparently thought of it as something radically different than its modern day interpreters. In fact the movement itself originated outside of the church, in England in the 1780's as a kind of literacy school, whose goals were mainly to deal with juvenile delinquents. This

---

[40] Lock E. Bowman, Jr., Don P. McGuirk, Donald L. Griggs, Gary L. DeVelder, Essential Skills for Good Teaching, Scotts- dale, Arizona: The Arizona Equipment, 1974), p. 1.

was obviously not a religious endeavor. The model then was one of an agency for social reform. This movement which was believed to be started by Robert

Raikes earned him the name of "the father of the Sunday School",[41] and brought him much recognition and acclaim. "All because he decided to educate poor children on the Lord's Day".[42]

The movement quickly spread throughout the English speaking world until it reached the New World where it under went some expansion to include new experiments in pluralism.

The differences in British and American Sunday Schools began to emerge in the 1820's. Despite the similarities in the evangelical point of view and the American borrowing, departures were inevitable in the New World. The first margin of difference was the constituencies. The early nineteenth century English Sunday Schools remained, for all practical purposes, institutions for children of the poor. Those in America became more inclusive.

This expansion was not without its repercussions,

---

[41] Lawrence M. Brammer, The Helping Relationship, (Engle- wood Cliffs, New Jersey: Prentice-Hall, Inc., 1979), p. 5.

[42] Joyce and Weil, Models of Teaching, p. XIX.

however, particularly in regard to racially prejudice attitudes.

The introduction of an inclusiveness cutting across white class lines made the presence of black children embarrassing and troublesome. Generally speaking, the American Sunday School movement faithfully observed the culture' caste demarcations just as English evangelicals reflected the class lines there.

Soon the expanded movement in the United States had adapted itself to its new environment and moved in to serve both the secular and the religious sector. It should be noted, however, that in the South, there was much opposition against the Sunday School Union mainly because of its efforts to educate blacks. This opposition increased even more after Nat Turner's rebellion.

Slave rebellions of the 1830's added a growing prejudice against Sunday Schools. It was known that Nat Turner's education was 'chiefly acquired in the Sunday Schools'. The text books for the small children were the ordinary speller and reader, and that for the older Negroes the Bible. Those planters who had ignored state prohibitions against teaching slaves were less inclined to do so when they saw Sunday School classes as potential breeding grounds for revolution and trouble.

In addition to it's sometimes image of patriotism, the Sunday School also became a forum for social issues. Eventually the combination of sacred and secular gave way to a predominant religious emphasis. Perhaps the Uniformed Lesson Series and the vision of Bible study on a mass scale were the greatest factors in moving to this strong religious emphasis. As the movement progressed, the Sunday School became more completely institutionalized and shaped by denomination. There were some attempts by so-called professionals who attempted to reform the movement, but it remained in the hands of lay-persons. Thus the movement of the Sunday School had reached its climax. This climax however, marked also the birth of new images and models. Among these is one described by Sarah Little which takes into account the recent decline experienced by many mainline denominations. According to Little the Sunday School is a "badly organized miracle".

The Theological Perspectives

It is in "Apologetic Theology" more so than any other that teaching in the church finds perhaps its greatest motive for doing what we do. The implications of this theological perspective are that the Christian community in the form of its teaching ministry must accept the responsibility for answering questions. This is not to say that our teaching must take on the tenor of recent attempts to defend the faith.

As Paul Tillich puts it:

> *The term 'apologetic' which had such high standing in the early church, has fallen into disrepute because of the methods employed in the abortive attempts to defend Christianity against attacks from modern humanism, naturalism and historicism.*

Rather it is to say that authentic apologetic theology must be based upon the "Kerygma." It is the Kerygma that has conveyed the heart of Christian apostolic preaching and gives our teaching efforts its basis and criterion. As we teach, we are communicating Christian faith, God's revelation in Jesus Christ hence, the Kerygma. Our teaching must not only be based upon the Kerygma however, it must be stated theologically. It has to make sense. It is also important to note that we teach in a context which essentially is the Christian community. Other agencies may teach about Christian faith, but it is the Christian community's responsibility to communicate faith itself. As it does so it has as its aim not only the task of facilitating personal involvement in the community of faith but also to help members of the community to realize their responsibility to become witnesses of that in various other realms of their calling. At the very heart of our teaching, is our focus on the person.

"Whether else Christian teaching may be, it is at its base personal in nature, that is it is concerned with response to and relation with God and with our fellow men".

The Pastoral Norms

Any pastor who takes his role seriously cannot refuse to take into account the fact that it naturally involves him or her in the teaching ministry of the church. What shape that involvement takes and to what extent is that involvement varies from church to church but the fact remains that no serious pastor can assume an attitude of ambivalence towards teaching in the Church setting. To a large extent the pastor must be a teacher. The scriptures give strong support to the idea that those who were deeply engrossed in proclaiming the gospel were equally involved in teaching. (Acts 2: lff) This is not to suggest that pastors should spread themselves out any thinner than their full schedules now take them. Rather it is to affirm that the pastor's role in the teaching ministry cannot be a passive one. The pastor must assume leadership in planning and carrying out the church's teaching ministry. This also suggests that the quality and methods of teaching efforts are the pastor's concerns as well. Chief among these concerns however is the pastor's role to affirm the foundations for the community's teaching ministry. No one will perceive this responsibility from the same vantage point as the pastor.

C. What is the Rationale for Including Helping Skills?

It is important to our discussion of the rationale for including helping skills in our teaching in the Church setting that we reaffirm an already established presupposition. As we have already established, effective teaching is not an inherent character of Church setting teachers in spite of the many natural teaching talents or gifts they may bring to the teaching tasks. The fact of the matter is effective teaching is an open-ended goal that we only reach in parts as we develop and acquire those skills needed to increase our effectiveness. In the words of Lock E. Bowman, Jr., "we learn to teach, and we can identify skills we need in order to do it more effectively".

1. What are Helping Skills?

If, as we have established, teachers in the church must acquire necessary skills in order to teach effectively, it is my contention that the skills most needed are helping skills. In order to define what are helping skills, however, we must establish a view of what we mean by helping.

Essentially when we use the term helping we do so in the sense that it describes what we do when we facilitate growth towards the personal goals and strengthen others' abilities to cope with life. What is also implicit in this view is the idea that helping means to focus on the needs of individuals. In other words, it is a personalized approach to teaching. At the same time, it involves some degree of responsibility on the part of the learner who is the person being helped.

Helping another human being is basically a process of enabling that person to grow in the directions that person chooses, to solve problems and to face crises. This process assumes the helpee is aware of alternatives and is willing to take responsibility for acting on an alternative. Helping involves facilitating awareness of such alternatives and assessing readiness to act. Help, however, should be defined mainly by the helpees, who select the goals of their own growth, and helpees who also determine whether they want help at all.

It must be stressed that the aim of helping is not to create any sense of dependency; rather its chief aim is to facilitate eventual self-sufficiency and responsibility.

2. What is the Relationship between Teaching and Helping Skills?

The relationship between teaching and helping skills can adequately be described as a combined strategy approach. Moreover, one may be correctly seen as a major component of the application of the other. Indeed in many ways, helping skills are related to teaching. In fact, it can be correctly stated that helping skills are an integral part of the teaching task. On the other hand, teaching is a part of the process of helping. As teaching more extensively uses a helping approach, it ceases to impose decisions upon or to determine goals for the learner. Thus teaching is helping to the extent that it functions as a process of helping the~ learner to make adjustments and decisions vital to his or her learning.

The assumption that the teacher is mainly a transmitter of in-formation ignores the psychological fact that learning can take place only when the learner actively seeks to solve recognized problems. To further the learning process, the teacher may do many things, such as establishing an appropriate setting, organizing learning experiences, working with a group or an individual to identify purposes, and relating experiences to background and helping to appraise results. Teaching is a process of guiding the learning of others.

When helping skills are employed, the teaching task becomes more facilitative as opposed to the older concept of directive teaching. In many ways, this early concept is giving way to the point of view that helping more accurately reflects the function of teaching. It should be noted however, that ensuing conflicts will occur when attempts to perpetuate traditional teaching are confronted with the recognized need for the teacher to become more sensitive to the needs of the students. On the one hand, traditional teaching has assumed the prerogatives of compulsion, direction, judgment, and punishment. At the same time, the helping approach accepts no responsibility for forcing individuals into predetermined patterns of learning.

The major factor that has caused teaching and helping skills to be forged into this integral relationship is the recognition that traditional teaching simply has not addressed the needs of the students.

3. What Are the Effects of Using Helping Skills?

When teachers in the church employ helping skills in their teaching they must be prepared and indeed look for certain outcomes as these skills are applied. Moreover, the teacher must have an awareness of which particular combination skills will bring about certain results or effects. For example, understanding and support skills are prominent in building levels of trust in a relationship. On the other hand, decision and action skills must be employed at some point, if learning is to take place. Still, helping must not only expect learning to take place but also resistance to learning. In addition to excitement and increased interest students at times, also experienced feelings of annoyance and discomfort when focus is centered on them or their particular needs.

a. The Instructional Effects

Perhaps the greatest outcome for the teachers themselves as they use helping skills is the personal satisfaction that student's curiosity and creativity is advanced and the natural desire to learn is subsequently enhanced. In short teachers no longer need to go through feelings of frustration and failure over the outcome of their teaching efforts.

b. Nurturant Effects

Among the nurturant effects from the use of helping skills, perhaps the freedom to experience learning in an environment that facilitates it looms large. Educators generally agree that students learn better when their interests are stimulated and their desires to explore are aroused.

Since education of all types including Christian education more and more is seeking to respond to the needs of the individuals, the use of helping skills is an effective way to address this desire. Such an approach not only increases the capacity of the learner to develop, but it also helps teachers develop more effective ways of relating to other human beings.

Upstream Analyses

What has come out of the requisites that I have put forth are some conclusions which contain certain imperatives for improving teaching in the church through the use of helping skills.

In my attempt to analyze the teaching efforts that take place in the church, I have drawn both from non-church related teaching resources and church related sources. While teaching in the church is obviously not identical to teaching in the public schools, it is equally obvious that we can ignore its similarities and resources only to our severe detriment. It is my conclusion that one cannot adequately define teaching in the Church setting until one defines teaching apart from its peculiar setting. When reduced to this point, an analysis of the dynamics of teaching in the Church setting is much easier to obtain.

Moreover when we consider the goals of our teaching efforts in the Church setting, namely those of helping learners to experience encounters with God and nurturing members in their Christian faith, as well as the need maximize our teaching efforts in the time allotted, it becomes increasingly clear that teacher effectiveness in the Church setting will not come by chance or as a result of having teachers who merely possess certain innate teaching talent. Thus we must conclude that only by acquiring the essential skills can teaching in the Church setting be carried out effectively. Unless the teacher in the Church setting can, through his or her facilitative efforts help learners to experience richer and fuller living, they are of little value as teachers.

A Test Case: Using the Strategies for Improving Teaching Through the Use of Helping Skills

If, as we have already concluded, traditional teaching in the Church setting, in terms of theory and practice warrants radical improvement, and because the specific type of improvement clearly involves being pro-active and the need for acquiring and using helping skills, it follows then that a test must be employed to assist teachers in the church to experience what it is like when teachers in the church employ this strategy.

The approach used in this case was mainly drawn to a very large degree from lessons learned by me from my previous experiences during the Teaching-Learning Process courses taken at Union theological seminary. I drew heavily from the syntax and strategies in the "Personal Family" models and the "Information Processing" models of teaching, as put forth by Joyce and Weil. Moreover, in testing out my thesis, I did indeed presuppose that there would be an imbalance between the nurturant effects and the instructional effects. This presupposition does require some degree of explanation, however.

It was felt that during the practicums that it was very important that the teachers themselves be open and consciously aware of their own feelings. The reason was that those teachers whose intent it was to create these nurturant effects among their students could increase their chances for success after having practiced it themselves.

It should be especially be noted that since there are many "helping skills" that could be taught, a choice had to be made as to which skills would be taught in these practicums. The choice was finally made in favor of listening and communication skills because both educators and education counsellors consider these skills to be not only basic to inter-personal relationships but also they considered them to be germane to any attempts to personalize the teaching-learning process.

A. The Prior Assumptions of Teachers

At First Baptist, teachers in the church meet twice a month on the first and third Wednesday evenings at seven o'clock (See Appendix L). These meetings are led by either the Church setting superintendent or my-self depending on the topic for discussion. The discussions themselves vary from formal to informal, again depending on the specific topic being discussed. At times the meeting would even take the shape of a formal class. This usually happens when I am teaching some new approach or technique. In general; however, the meetings take the form of discussion whose purposes are: to evaluate the effectiveness of present teaching strategies; to share experiences of teachers and students during teaching-learning activities; to share approaches to future lessons; to evaluate teaching methods; to express needs, concerns, failures or frustrations experienced in teaching efforts.

It was during our regular Wednesday evening

Teacher's meeting that the teachers in the church indicated that they were having serious problems attempting to address the needs and interests of their students. As the discussions on this subject progressed the teachers were led by me into an awareness that they needed to move more in the direction of "personalizing" their teaching efforts. The aim of my efforts was to cause the teachers to begin thinking about teaching in the Church setting as a way of relating to their students. Moreover, I wanted them to visualize themselves as being more in the roles of helpers and facilitators and less in the roles of biblical authorities and dispensers of religious information.

1. What Were the Teacher's Assumptions About Expanding Their Teaching Methods?

While the teacher's feelings were mostly positive towards my efforts to get them to think differently about their teaching efforts, in their judgment the limited amount of time available for them to get their lessons across would not permit them to use any other approach. In other words, one of their assumptions was that personalizing required time far beyond that which is allotted to the teaching activities during Church setting. It was also assumed by the teachers that personalizing, that is becoming helpers and facilitators of learning, was a method in and of itself.

At this point I asked the teachers in the church to think about their present teaching methods in terms of its effectiveness in focusing on the needs and interest of the learners. Then the discussion moved to determining what was needed in order for teachers to become more effective. While all of the teachers were surprisingly self-critical of their present teaching methods and agreed that something was needed, none of the teachers were ready to concede that a totally different method was the answer. In this discussion it was revealed that the teachers assumed that an increase in effective- ness would likely mean total elimination of present teaching methods that they had adopted and developed over a period of time and have become very comfortable in using. When I suggested that the effectiveness of their present methods could be greatly expanded and improved upon, their initial reaction was mixed with doubt and suspicion.

It should also be noted that a major assumption made by the teachers in the church had to do with the curriculum that they were currently using. Presently most of the teachers were using curriculum that was published by a national Publishing Board on the International Sunday School lesson. While the material gives extensive, though very conservative, biblical exposition, it does very little to assist teachers in preparing their lessons. For example there are no "suggested teaching activities", no clearly identified lesson concepts, objectives or goals. When I shared the chapter "Ten Curriculum Decisions Teachers Must Make" from the book "Teaching Teachers to Teach" by Donald L. Griggs, I discovered that the teachers were under the assumption that they must cover all the material presented in the lesson. They obviously were unable to do this because of limited amounts of time allotted to them for teaching but this did not deter most of them from making a valiant attempt each Sunday morning. As a result, when the bell sounded calling a halt to their teaching activities, these teachers usually began entertaining feelings of frustration and failure. It was clear in their minds that the strategy of the teachers, for getting the information out took precedence over any attempt to focus on the needs and interests of the students. At the same time, the teaching activities were clearly one-sided in favor of mostly cognitive objectives such as the memorization of names and places or the understanding of certain terms or concepts.

2. The Teacher's Assumptions about Helping Skills?

As I have previously stated, most of the teachers in the church were under the assumption that they must cover all of the material contained in the curriculum used. This, in turn, also led to the assumption that their lesson goals must be more general and broad enough to include this vast body of material. Hence, as they readily admitted, it was extremely difficult to properly assess to what degree their teaching efforts had reached the needs and interests of the students. At the same time, the teachers felt that there was even less of a possibility of analyzing learner interactions. In other words, the objectives of the teachers in the test church were heavily content and fact oriented. For this reason, most of the teachers assumed that the incorporation of helping skills would undermine their effectiveness in reaching these objectives. Furthermore it was assumed that since incorporation of helping skills called for them to talk less and listen more, this would also mean they would lose valuable teaching time. In like manner, it was assumed that allowing students more freedom to interact and express themselves would subsequently result in a loss of control of the time and the content of student response. On the other hand, the teacher assumed that there was a very real possibility that giving the students more freedom to verbalize their feelings could have an adverse effect upon other students or upon the tenor of the entire class. As one teacher expressed it, "I wanted to try it one morning but I was afraid that if some of the students became upset, I would never be able to get the class to settle down again".

As I stated before, the teachers were generally in agreement that something needed to be done to improve their teaching effectiveness as well as to increase the student's interest. What the teachers assumed however, was that an improvement in their ability to give out more information would, in turn, create more interest among the students. For this reason, then the teachers' perception of their needs was that they needed more teaching time, not more teaching skills. In other words, they did not perceive the incorporation of helping skills as crucial to their teaching effectiveness.

It should be noted at this point that all of our teachers in the church except one are education majors and have had experience teaching in the public schools. The one who is not an education major does teach in a job related capacity. In other words, all of our teachers have had teaching experience other than teaching in the Church setting. I did not find it strange then, that they all had some awareness of the concept than others. Some, in fact, were only vaguely aware of its meaning under a different name. Ironically so, none of the teachers seemed to have an awareness that helping skills can or should be seen as a major component of their teaching methods. Their assumptions were that helping skills, if they belong to a teaching environment at all, surely did not belong in the Church setting teaching activities. On the contrary, they saw these skills as related mainly to those methods employed on the level of special education classes. In other words, the teachers saw helping skills as being those skills employed in those classes held for students with learning disabilities or at the most those skills that could be employed in classes with a longer period for teaching activities.

Some of the teachers who saw the potential value of helping skills in other types of teaching efforts such as leadership training or membership classes were still skeptical about the value of helping skills in dealing with typical Church setting curriculums. That is, the Church setting teacher's perception of biblically oriented materials such as the Sunday School curriculum was that it should be treated first and foremost as information to be memorized and conceptualized. While some attempts were made, time permitting, to reflect upon the content of the material, very little priority was given to relating the lesson to the needs or interests of the students. This was especially true of teachers of youth and children. The typical question asked in the period given for summarizing the lesson for that day was, "What was today's lesson about?" not, what meaning did the lesson have for your life? or how did the lesson affect your life, attitude or behavior? While the teachers did not indicate a complete disregard for the student's interests, abilities to be creative or their needs to ex- press themselves, it is clear that they did not feel that these were important enough to warrant a place in the major focus of the teaching activities. In short, they considered themselves as being much more comfortable assuming the roles of processors of learning and dispensers of information, than assuming the roles of helpers and facilitators.

Perhaps it would be helpful here to summarize the assumptions of the teachers in the church at First Baptist. From our informal discussions in the regular Wednesday evening teacher's meeting I have discovered that:

1. The teachers believed that personalizing or changing their focus from lesson centering to person centering requires more than the allotted time given to teaching activities.
2. The teachers believed that becoming helper or facilitators of learning meant getting rid of their present teaching methods and adopting a new method.
3. The teachers believed that using helping skills is a teaching method apart from other methods.
4. The teachers were fearful that using helping skills would jeopardize their ability to control

the teaching time and undermine their ability to cover all of the lesson material.

5. That the teachers felt threatened by the possibility of giving more freedom for verbal and creative expressions.

It is obvious that some of the Church setting teacher's assumptions were directly related to their views on planning for the lesson and only in- directly related to their views on helping skills.

For example, their views about covering all of the curriculum clearly stems from a failure to understand that in planning for their lessons the teacher, and not the curriculum writer, must decide how much material will be covered. More- over, the teacher's assumptions seem to indicate that they did not actually plan for student involvement beyond merely answering questions or reciting information from memory. In fact, it appeared that the teachers felt more comfortable when they were exercising greater control over their student's responses. Perhaps the most revealing discovery made from the teacher's assumptions was the tremendous weight and focus upon the written curriculum material as opposed to a student centered focus. In other words, their objectives seemed to be not how much took place but how much material was presented.

B. What Action Was Taken to Relate Helping Skills to Teaching?

The action taken during this project to relate help-ing skills to teaching was based essentially on the as-sumptions made by the teachers in the church of First Baptist and my own perceptions on what was needed to improve their teaching through the use of helping skills.

Based upon the assumptions made by the teachers in the church, it was determined that the fundament-tall cause of teacher's attitudes and feelings toward the use of helping skills was their partial and, in some cases, their total lack of understanding about helping skills. In other words, they lacked under- standing of what helping skills were and, most of all, how they were to be used in their teaching-learning activities. Essentially then, we were dealing not only with the need to train teachers in the use of helping skills but it also became our task to correct a false perception held by the teach-ers of the relationship of helping skills to the teaching task. As it has already been stated, those teachers who were at least familiar with the concept, helping skills, still viewed the employment of these skills as being extraneous to the task of teaching. To assume the roles of facilitator or helper in their minds was to become something other than a teacher and consequently to be involved in some- thing other than teaching. At the same time, I was aware that, at least, in the case of the experienced public school teachers, that I was dealing with a particular tendency to focus heavily upon the lesson or at least upon the information that it contained, rather than on the learners. Thus, it became my task, in this phase of the project, to address these attitudes and actions which I was convinced needed either to be changed and/or improved upon by teaching the teachers in a workshop setting, using various teaching methods, two of the recognized basic helping skills.

1. What Were the Project Goals?

The goals pursued in this project, in order to relate helping skills to teaching, fell into three categories; namely, performance, attitude and skills. The goals were:

Performance Goals - Session #1

1. That teachers become more conscious of how their own self- understanding paves the way for their use of helping skills.
2. That teachers come to realize the importance of being able not only to hear words but to interpret expressions of feelings, concern and values.
3. That teachers become more aware of the potential for distractions when one is listening.
4. That teachers understand what is needed in order for students to become better followers of directions.
5. That teachers recognize the need to teach students how to distinguish between different types of information.

Performance Goals - Session #2

1. That teachers become more aware of what is effective communication.
2. That teachers become more conscious of the various types of constructive and destructive communications.

3. That teachers realize the importance of how one communicates.

4. That teachers become more conscious of how persons speak non-verbally.

5. That teachers become better able to recognize when defense mechanisms are being used.

Attitudinal Goals - Session #1

1. That teachers recognize the importance of attentiveness.

2. That teachers realize the need to continue to sharpen their ability to hear what students are saying.

Attitudinal Goals - Session #2

1. That teachers become more able to verbally interact in a more open and sincere manner.

2. That teachers realize how the way they communicate can block communication.

Skills Goals - Session #1

1. That teachers become more aware of what it takes to follow directions.
2. That teachers recognize the importance of separating facts from ideas.
3. That teachers become better able to understand the expressions they hear and see.

Skills Goals - Session #2

1. That teachers understand the importance of good feedback.
2. That teachers realize how important it is for students to be heard.
3. That teachers recognize the value of support and praise.

What Were the Project Objectives? (see Appendix D-E)

The objectives, like the goals of the project, fell into three categories, which were performance, attitude and skills.

Performance Objectives - Session #1

At the end of the Session, participants should be able to:

1. As a result of a personal inventory assessment (see Appendix A), identify personal listening skills that need improvement.

2. Given a group of cartoons for interpretation, recognize expressions of concern, feelings and values.

3. After listening to a tape, identify descriptive words, comparisons and be able to summarize pertinent information from a conversation.

4. As a result of direct instruction, implement the techniques of following directions by drawing a symmetrical design based upon stated directions.

5. Distinguish between facts and ideas by writing a brief summary from what was overheard during the listening session.

Performance Objectives - Session #2

At the end of the Session participants should be able to:

1. As a result of listening to three taped examples, and subsequent test, summarize information, separate fact from fiction and recognize feelings behind words.

2. As a result of listening to taped sessions, distinguish between dialogue (an exchange of ideas and opinions between two or more persons) and duologue (a dialogue between two persons and identify types of non-verbal communication.

3. Given the listing of "Speech Mannerisms" and listening to conversation by two participants, identify various speech mannerisms employed in conversations.

4. After brainstorming for body idioms, identify ways in which we use our bodies to express feelings.

5. After role playing from identity cards, identify feelings of attacking and being attacked.

Attitudinal Objectives - Session #1

At the end of this Session the attitudes of the participants towards listening should be expressed in:

1. Their need to be more attentive as a listener.
2. Their need to recognize that good listening is a skill that needs continual development and refinement.

Attitudinal Objectives - Session #2

At the end of this Session the attitudes of participants towards communication should be expressed in:

1. Their need to communicate with honesty.
2. Their awareness that our mannerism can either hinder or help our communication.

Skills Objectives - Session #1

At the end of this Session, participants should have acquired skills in:

1. Following directions.
2. Distinguishing between facts and ideas.
3. Recognizing expressions of feelings and values.

Skills Objectives - Session #2

At the end of this Session, participants should have skills in:

1. Identifying and speaking to feelings.
2. Concentration on what is being said.
3. Helping students to share positive feelings.

What Strategy Was Utilized?

The strategy utilized to relate helping skills to Teaching in Session #1 was as follows (see Appendix D):

The strategy used in this session was basically deductive. The workshop duration was two and one half hours long and the primary resource was a kit entitled "Learning to Listen". The content outline was as follows (see Appendix D):

I. The Characteristics of a Good Listener

II. Listening for Evidence of Feelings

III. Listening for Specific Responses

IV. Listening for Directions

Opening and Presenting the Subject

Shortly after the opening and prior to presenting the subject teachers were given a personal inventory to fill out.

Teachers were given direct instructions on the concepts of teachings and helping skills. Comparisons were made between teaching without helping skills and teaching with helping skills. Comparisons were also made between the teaching objectives of the two types of teaching. A list of characteristics of a good listener was given to the participants and a discussion on the personal inventory followed. Teachers were then asked to verbalize ways in which they felt they could improve their listening skills as they engaged in their teaching activities.

Teachers were given a list of barriers to good listening. A further discussion on the inventory followed using this list.

Exploring the Subject

Teachers now engaged in direct involvement (hands on) working individually through cartoons, identifying the feelings expressed by these cartoons, the concerns and values.

Responding Creatively

Teachers further engaged in direct involvement, expressing themselves by writing brief summaries of taped messages which gives descriptive words, comparisons, directions, ideas and facts. The participants must listen well and distinguish each category.

Closing the Session

Teachers shared in this period individually and in pairs the subjects covered and how this impacted on their teaching methods and their previous attitudes. The teachers were asked to carefully fill out an evaluation of the session. The session was closed with prayer.

The strategy utilized to relate helping skills to teaching in Session #2 was as follows (see Appendix E):

The strategy for this session was basically deductive. The workshop duration was two and one half hours long and the primary resource was a kit entitled "Effective Communication". The content outline was as follows (see Appendix E):

I. The Art of Listening
II. Awareness of Feelings
III. Speech Mannerisms and Body Talk
IV. Attacking and Defending

Opening and Presenting the Subject

The session opened with a brief period of direct instruction on the relationship of helping skills to teaching as a rationale for the session.

Teachers were then engaged in direct involvement, listening to examples on tape that focused on listening skills. Teachers continued listening to examples on tape of commercials, group discussions and directions that were given.

These were done to emphasize the need to be attentive in listening to expressions.

Exploring the Subject

The teachers continued to engage in direct involvement this time inductively discovering the difference between duologue and dialogue. They also discovered inductively how a person communicated non-verbally by observing a wordless conversation held by two of the participants. The teachers ended their exploring activity by engaging in the age old "Rumor Game". They discovered as many others have done that people who do not listen well are not able to repeat what is said to them and a communication break-down occurs.

Responding Creatively

Teachers now engage in individual reflections about the session. Afterwards the teachers are given instructions to clarify their expressions and also to write down feelings that they experience daily. Teachers are then asked to share these feelings with other participants.

Teachers now engage in group direct involvement, brainstorming for speech and body mannerisms which they either use themselves or observed in others. They discuss what these mannerisms do to communication. Teachers also engage in a series of role playing exercises in order to increase their knowledge of body language. Teachers end this portion with exercises in verbal attacks and defense mechanisms.

Closing the Session

The closing of the session began in small groups who shared what effects the two sessions have had on their approach to teaching. The teachers further shared how they felt these newly acquired helping skills would be employed in their future teaching efforts. There was further sharing with the entire group from a representative from each small group. An evaluation was done and the session was closed in prayer.

C. The Analysis of the Project

The analysis of the project involves a critical look at what essentially took place during the two workshops through the eyes of the participants and through my own eyes. It is a critical look both in the sense that evaluative instruments were used (see Appendix and in the sense that an attempt was made through these instruments to gain honest but critical feedback from the participants. The names of those who filled out the evaluative instruments remained anonymous, however, they were asked to indicate the particular position they held in the church. From the evaluation, instruments compilations were made both of the comments themselves and the frequency of those comments (see Appendix H). From these instruments, an attempt was made to accurately assess/ where the participants were in terms of their prior knowledge of the subject, what value the workshops had for the participants themselves, what impact the workshops had on the participant's performance as teachers, and what impact the workshops had upon the participant's attitude towards teaching. At the same time the participants were asked to evaluate my performance and the instruments reflected their assessment of how I conducted myself as we moved through the phase of each workshop. Lastly, the participants were allowed to give general comments in the way of suggestions and/or criticisms of either the workshop itself or the conductor.

1. The Teacher's Evaluation of the Project

The teacher's evaluation consists, first of all, of their assessment of each workshop through the use of a teaching session evaluation instrument (see Appendixes I and J). These forms were given out just prior to the closing of each session to all of the participants. It should be noted that all but approximately four participants turned in their evaluation forms. Those participants who did not participate in the evaluation were persons who missed significant portions of the workshops and therefore, did not feel that they could give a fair assessment.

When the evaluations were all in, a compilation was made in two parts. First, there was a compilation made of the rating scale evaluations (see Appendixes F and G). Secondly, there was a compilation made of the general comments made either in answer to specific questions or in response to the request made to give additional comments/suggestions (see Appendix H).

The compilations of Workshop #1 revealed that, out of the nine participants who participated in the evaluation, four gave the workshop the highest rating (5) in terms of its in-formativeness and four others gave a (4). One participant gave a "no report". In general then, the teachers rated the workshop very high in terms of its content and the knowledge gained from it. In the area of interests (thought-provoking) eight of the nine participants gave the highest rating (5) and one gave a fair rating (3). In general, the teachers found the workshop to hold their interests and attention as it moved throughout the various phases.

In terms of the workshop's pragmatic value, five of the nine participants gave the workshop the highest rating (5), three rated the workshop (4) and one participant did not report in this area. In general, then, the majority of the teachers found the workshop to be very good in terms of its practical value to them as teachers. In the area of shortness of time, one participant gave the highest (4), while five of the participants gave an average rating of (3). Two other participants gave no report in this area. What this seems to suggest, in the opinion of the participants, is that the workshop length was adequate but could have been longer.

The teacher's ratings of the workshop conductor for Workshop #1 indicated that, in the area of preparedness, six of the nine participants gave' me the highest rating (5), two gave me the next highest (4) and one rated me average (3). In general then the teachers considered me to be very well prepared for what I did. In terms of my response to the participants' questions, seven out of the nine participants gave me the highest rating (5) and two rated me average (3). This suggests to me that on a whole, I did an excellent job of answering questions but on at least a couple of questions my answers were not perceived to be that good. On my ability to hold the interests of the participants, four out of the nine gave me the highest rating (5), four of the other participants gave me the second highest rating (4) and one gave me an average rating (3). In general, this suggests that I was able to maintain interest at a very high level throughout the workshop.

The compilations of Workshop #2 revealed ratings much more favorable than in Workshop #1. In my judgement, the reasons were twofold. First of all the workshop itself had many more direct involvement (hands on) activities than the previous Work- shop #1. This seems to imply that students gain more enjoyment out of those classes where they are involved in activities. Obviously, all teaching activities cannot be of this nature but there seems to be a definite correlation here. Secondly, the teachers, by now, are becoming more aware of the value of helping skills to their teaching efforts. In short they are beginning to see that helping skills have an integral relationship to teaching.

The compilations of Workshop #2 reveal that seven out of the ten participants of this workshop gave the workshop the highest rating (5), in terms of its in formativeness, and three gave it the second highest rating (4). This seems to indicate that teachers overwhelmingly considered the content of the workshop and the knowledge gained from it to be very high to excellent. In the area of interest (thought provoking) seven out of the ten gave the workshop the highest rating (5), one gave the workshop the next highest rating (4) and two participants did not report on this area. It is unknown why these two did not give a report on this area but again the overwhelming consideration seems to be that the workshop was highly thought provoking. In terms of its practical value four of the participants gave the workshop the highest rating, five gave it the second highest rating (4) and one gave no report on this area. This seems to suggest that the teachers found this workshop equally as helpful as the first to their teaching methods. In terms of the shortness of workshop, one participant rated it second highest (4), seven of the others rated it average (3) and two gave no report on this area. This seems to suggest that the length of this workshop was very good.

The teacher's ratings of the workshop conductor for Workshop #2 indicated that in the area of preparedness six participants gave me the highest rating (5), and the remaining four gave me the second highest rating (4). They seemed to say "in the area of readiness I am very good". As far as my response to the participant's questions, five of the teachers gave me the highest rating (5), four of the others gave me the second highest rating (4) and one did not report in this area. Perhaps the brightest spot of this particular evaluation came in the area of my ability to hold the interests of the participants during the work- shop. In this area nine out of the ten participants' gave me the highest rating (5) and one gave me the second highest rating (4). As I pointed out before, there were more direct involvement (hand on) activities in this workshop and the teacher's rating seems to reflect that fact.

As I previously stated, in addition to the rating scale evaluations, a compilation of the general comments were made. In making this compilation, the comments and/or criticisms were grouped according to their frequency (see Appendix H). The chart shows the type of comments made and the (X) indicates each time the comment was made. To summarize, there seemed to be a great deal of support in favor of having these workshops more frequently. There also seemed to be some support for having other types of workshops as well. While the other comments (helpful, greater clarification, need for greater participation, alter-native approaches, shorter sessions, more frequent sessions) did not occur with any noteworthy degree of frequency they do indicate areas I need to look at for possible improvement.

2. My Evaluation of the Project

In making my assessment of the project I attempted to construct an evaluation instrument that would give me an outline to examine not only what happened but possibly why it happened. Much of the instrument was borrowed from an instrument used by Dr. Little in a Teaching and Education class. While the form does not meet my total satisfaction, it goes a long way toward providing me with the instrument that I am looking for. First of all, the project, in general, was held on the times and dates scheduled (see Appendix J). The weather was good which seemed to favor good attendance at both workshops. As I stated earlier there were some participants who could not take full advantage of the workshops but on a whole those who committed themselves remained throughout.

In reviewing the plan, I have determined that I was able to follow it very close to the way it was originally written. I did find however, that I had to give some teaching activities less time than originally planned in order to stay within the time allotted. As interest increased so did the number of questions that were raised. This also seemed to take up more time than anticipated. I suppose the greatest reason the plan worked so well is the fact that Dr. Little persuaded me to clarify my objectives. Once these became clear, it was not too demanding to come up with a work- able plan. I could not have asked for more relevant resources than the two kits I used. They were tailor-made for both their content and their topic. Since these helping skills were basic helping skills they were just what I needed for those who had very little prior knowledge of their relationship to teaching.

During the teaching sessions, because the interest

and attention levels were so high the flow was very rapid at times. Not only did the teachers enjoy the group work but they seemed anxious to share their thoughts and feelings. On one or two occasions, I sensed that some participants had moved to very deep levels of feelings. I was at a lost as to how to handle this without causing undue attention to be drawn to those persons.

My teaching during the session, I would judge to be on target in terms of my ability to feel comfortable with using various types of teaching methods and strategies. I knew what I was doing most of the time mainly because I had just completed the teaching-learning class. In spite of my bias in favor of using helping skills, I still find myself talking too much when I am asked a question.

On a whole, it is my feeling that the project was very successful in terms of holding the teacher's interests and involving them in the teaching activities. There were enough activities of a volunteer nature that I had no trouble getting those who were somewhat shy actively involved. Perhaps the only reaction that troubled me was the initial reaction of the teachers to the personal inventory (see Appendix A). In retrospect,

I realize that this called for too radical a revealing of oneself that most of us avoid on a regular basis. On future occasions I would do more to prepare participants for activities of this nature.

D. What Have I Learned?

What I have come to realize as I moved through the phases of this project falls essentially in three categories. These categories are: what I have learned about teacher's assumptions about "helping skills", what I have learned about introducing new concepts, and what developmental changes can take place between the geneses of a new idea and when it reaches the workable stage.

Much to my surprise, I found that the idea of using helping skills in teaching is still a relatively new idea to several teachers who have been teaching in the public schools. Among those who are familiar with the idea, the implementation still appears to be threatening. Moreover, the personalized focus required by its implementation still causes them to believe that this belongs to another setting other than the normal classroom. Still what I have learned and witnessed, especially the teaching-learning activities of the workshops, is that, like teaching in the public schools, the strength of teaching in the Church setting will be in its ability to use a variety of approaches. I am convinced that one of the best approaches that will enable teachers in the church to create learning environments that are conducive to the process of stimulating, examining and evaluating new concepts and perceptions of Christian faith is an approach that incorporates "helping skills".

What I have also learned however, is that introducing new concepts in teaching, like introducing new concepts in Christian faith is often a gradual painstaking process. I have learned about this endeavor, as I have learned in various other phases of my ministry career that others do not necessarily share the same excitement and enthusiasm that I do about a new idea regardless of its pragmatic value. I have certainly learned that it is incumbent upon those of us who are responsible for the direction and quality of our teaching in the Church setting, to be thorough in our planning, patient in our implementation, flexible in our strategy and precise in our aims and objectives as we introduce new concepts. A new idea that is rejected rarely gets an immediate second chance to be presented.

Perhaps the most difficult lesson for me has been the recognition that new ideas, like creation itself must undergo developmental stages before some workable order can come out of the original chaos. This, like introducing a new idea, is a painstaking process. In this case however, the pain is much more intense. The pain of research, testing out theories, drawing conclusions, evaluating, analyzing data to mention only a few, was excruciating to say the least. But as one catches the glimmer of a new creation it all becomes worthwhile. In relation to this awareness, I also must admit that this creation is not complete, nor does it have a monopoly on creative acts. We have not reached the pinnacle in improving our teaching in the church school. Perhaps Robert Schaefer said it best in his foreword to Bruce Joyce and Marsha Weil's book, "Models of Teaching:"

There is no royal freeway to pedagogical success, no painless solution to complex instructional problems and no future in our persistent effort to describe the best teaching practice.

III

Possibilities and Future Implications

It has certainly occurred to me that what has been done to improve teaching in the Church setting cannot and should not be confined to any one setting alone. On the contrary, since teaching is obviously not confined to any venue in the Church setting, it follows that no improvement of teaching can be restricted to any particular domain. This means that helping skills can and should be employed throughout the church's teaching ministry.

A. The Possibilities for Further Expansion in Teaching Methods

As I stated earlier, the listening and communicative helping skills are basic helping skills, but at the same time they are only two of many other helping skills. They are confronting skills, paraphrasing skills, leading skills, interpreting skills, informing skills, crisis skills and summarizing skills, just to name a few that all fall under the category of helping skills. Consequently, the possibilities for expanding our teaching methods to include these skills seem almost endless. Moreover, as in the case of listening and communicative skills, many helping skills are related to each other. This means that as one acquires skill in one there is a very real possibility the skills are sharpened in those related skills. On the other hand, as one sharpens and subsequently uses that skill there should be an increased awareness of the need to sharpen those skills related to the use of that skill. For example, one cannot be an attentive listener without regard to the need to communicate well in paraphrasing and clarifying what has been heard. What this also suggests is that helping skills should be acquired in related combinations rather than in isolation of one another.

Notwithstanding, at First Baptist the point needs to be driven home that helping skills can and should be incorporated in the teaching task regard- less of the method or the content of the particular lesson.

Even when dealing with detailed biblical facts or the concepts of the Christian faith, learning is better facilitated when teachers use helpful skills. This is not to deny that some teaching methods lend themselves more to helping skills than others. At the same time, however we must recognize that we seldom use the same method throughout our teaching efforts. While methodology does make a difference in how and what kind of learning takes place, the incorporation of helping skills in many instances makes the difference in how much is learned and how motivated the learner will be toward the learning process. It is a recognized fact among educators that methodology alone does not ensure that learning will take place.

Thus, at First Baptist, and for that matter teachers in the church anywhere, who are operating under the assumption that helping skills are a method in and of themselves must now see that there is an integral relationship between helping skills and teaching. This means that helping skills should not be seen by the teachers as options or extras that they may incorporate at their leisure. On the contrary, helping skills must be seen as major components of all teaching methodologies and therefore their use become an imperative.

Since no learning can take place apart from the person who is the object of our teaching efforts then no teaching should take place apart from our strong desire to personalize those efforts. It is my contention that the incorporation of helping skills in teaching methods in the Church setting will make the difference between a badly organized boring routine and what Sarah Little has deemed to be a "badly organized miracle".

B. The Possibilities Implicit in Other Teaching Efforts

If, in fact, helping skills should not be confined to teaching efforts in the Church setting alone, then that suggests that helping skills stems from a common thread that runs throughout the church's entire teaching ministry. For Christian educators at least, that common thread has to do with the motive for our ministering actions. It is the common thread that places upon Christian educators of all types the responsibility to engage in caring for others and the sharing of themselves as they teach. It is my belief that the use of helping skills in their teaching provides a more than suitable means for carrying out this responsibility. While I have been specific in showing how this is true about teaching in the Church setting, I am convinced that it is also true of other types of teaching efforts.

For example, because the use of helping skills has a greater impact upon the teacher's ability to enter the learners own frame of reference and to facilitate his or her personal growth and understanding, then it seems to me that this use of helping skills has wide spread possibilities in small group teaching settings and in the area of educative counseling. In small group settings such as age group fellowships, leadership classes, committee meetings, new membership classes and organizational workshops there are persons involved whose needs and interests must be spoken to. The same is also true of preventative educative counseling which may take the form of pre- marital, preretirement, death and dying classes whose aim is to focus upon the needs of the participants. What is significant about these teaching efforts is that the main focus is not on the content or the subject that is being taught but the learner's needs, abilities and interests and the goal is to enhance the individual's growth and development.

Bibliography

Adams, Sam and John L. Garrett, Jr. To Be A Teacher. Englewood Cliffs, New Jersey: Prentice-Hall, Inc., 1969.

Berne, Eric. Principles of Group Treatment. New York: Grove Press, Inc., 1966.

Betts, George Herbert. How to Teach Religion. New York: The Abingdon Press, 1919.

Blazier, Kenneth D. Building An Effective Church setting. Valley Forge; Judson Press, 1976.

Blazier, Kenneth D. The Teaching Church at Work. Pennsylvania: Judson Press, 1980.

Boehlke, Robert R. Theories of Learning in Christian Education. Philadelphia: The Westminster Press, 1952.

Bowman, Locke E., Jr. Straight Talk About Teaching in Today's Church. Philadelphia: The Westminster Press, 1967.

Bowman, Locke E., Jr., Donn P. McGuirk, Donald L. Griggs and Gary L. DeVelder. Essential Skills for Good Teaching. Scottsdale: National Teacher Education Project, 1974.

Brammer, Lawrence M. The Helping Relationship. Englewood Cliffs, N. J.; Prentice-Hall, Inc., 1979.

Carkhuff, Robert R. and Bernard G. Berenson. Teaching as Treatment. Massachusetts: Human Resource Development Press, Inc., 1976.

Clinebell, Howard J., Jr. Basic Types of Pastoral Counseling. Nashville: Abingdon Press, 1966.

Cloud, Henry. Changes That Heal, Zondervan, Grand Rapids, Michigan 1992.

Ericksen, Stanford C. Motivation for Learning. Ann Arbor: The University of Michigan Press, 1974.

Freire, Paulo. Pedagogy of the Oppressed. New York: The Continuum Publishing Corporation, 1981.

Greeves, Frederic. Theology and the Cure of Souls. Manhasset, N. Y.; Channel Press, Inc., 1962.

Griggs, Donald L. Teaching Teachers to Teach. Livermore, Ca.: Griggs Educational Service, 1974.

Groome, Thomas H. Christian Religious Education. San Francisco: Harper and Row, Publishers, 1980.

Hilgard, Ernest R., Richard C. Atkinson and Rita L Atkinson. Introduction to Psychology. New York: Harcourt, Brace, Jovanovich, Inc., 1971.

Howe, Leland W. and Mary Martha Howe. Personalizinq Education. New York: A & W Visual Library, 1975.

Joyce, Bruce and Marsha Weil. Models of Teaching. New Jersey: Prentice-Hall, Inc., 1980.

Kemp, C. Gratton, Foundations of Group Counseling. New York: McGraw-Hill Book Company, 1970.

Kunkel, Fritz. In Search of Maturity. New York: Charles Scribner's Sons, 1943.

Lloyd-Jones, Esther M. and Norah Rosenau. Social and Cultural Foundations of Guidance. New York: Holt, Rinehart and Winston, Inc., 1968.

Lynn, Robert W. and Elliott Wright. The Big Little School. Birmingham, Alabama: Religious Education Press, 1980.

McLester, Frances C. Teaching in the Church setting. New York: Abingdon Press, 1961.

Miller, T. Franklin, Beverly Welton, James Blair Miller, Harold Johnson and Kenneth F. Hall. Basics for Teaching. Anderson, Indiana: Warner Press, Inc., 1968.

Olson, Richard Allen. The Pastor's Role in Educational Ministry. Philadelphia: Fortress Press, 1974.

Raths, Louis E., Merrill Harmin and Sidney B. Simon. Values and Teaching. Columbus, Ohio: Charles E. Merrill Publishing Co., 1966.

Rogers, Carl R. Client-Centered Therapy. Boston: Houghton Mifflin Co., 1965.

Rogers, Carl R. On Encounter Groups. New York: Harper & Row, Publishers, 1970.

Rogers, Carl R. Freedom to Learn for the 80's. Columbus: Charles E. Merrill Publishing Company, 1983.

Seymour, Jack L., Donald E. Miller, Sarah P. Little, Charles R. Foster, Allen J. Moore and Carol A. Wehrheim. Contemporary Approaches to Christian Education. Nashville: Abington, 1982.

Stiles, Lindley J. and Mattie F. Dorsey. Democratic Teaching in Secondary Schools. Chicago: J. B. Lippencott Company, 1950.

Taylor, Marvin J. An Introduction to Christian Education. Nashville: Abingdon Press, 1966.

Tillich, Paul. Systematic Theology, Vol. I Chicago: The University of Chicago Press, 1951.

Vieth, Paul H. How to Teach in the Church setting. Philadelphia: The Westminster Press, 1935.

Wyckoff, D. Campbell. The Task of Christian Education. Philadelphia: The Westminster Press, 1955.

Yalom, Ivin D. The Theory and Practice of Group Psychotherapy. New York: Basic Books, Inc., 1975.

Ziegler, Jesse H. Psychology and the Teaching Church. New York: Abingdon Press, 1962.

Appendixes

About the Author

While engaged in graduate studies my pastoral care load became overwhelming. I also realized some of the subjects I was studying and the issues I addressed during counseling were covered in my midweek Bible study sessions. Consequently, skills for intervention as well as theological rationale were acquired. When I shared this with my iconic Christian Education professor, Dr. Sarah Little. she said to me, "Tom I believe you have something here!"

Printed in the United States
By Bookmasters